The Birder

BIRD WATCHING LOG,
NOTEBOOK AND JOURNAL

A bird sitting on a tree
is never afraid
of the branch breaking,
because her trust
is not on the branch
but on her own wings.

BELONGS TO: _____

Notes / Bird Photo:

Bird Photo / Sketch:

Date:

Location:

Habitat:

GPS Co-ordinates:

Weather Conditions:

Birds Spotted / Quantity:

Birds Seen but Not Identified:
(Description)

Interesting Events:

Video Images Taken:
(File Name)

Notes / Bird Photo:

Bird Photo / Sketch:

Date:

Location:

Habitat:

GPS Co-ordinates:

Weather Conditions:

Birds Spotted / Quantity:

Birds Seen but Not Identified:
(Description)

Interesting Events:

Video Images Taken:
(File Name)

Notes / Bird Photo:

Bird Photo / Sketch:

Date:

Location:

Habitat:

GPS Co-ordinates:

Weather Conditions:

Birds Spotted / Quantity:

Birds Seen but Not Identified:
(Description)

Interesting Events:

Video Images Taken:
(File Name)

Notes / Bird Photo:

Bird Photo / Sketch:

Date:

Location:

Habitat:

GPS Co-ordinates:

Weather Conditions:

Birds Spotted / Quantity:

Birds Seen but Not Identified:
(Description)

Interesting Events:

Video Images Taken:
(File Name)

Notes / Bird Photo:

Bird Photo / Sketch:

Date:

Location:

Habitat:

GPS Co-ordinates:

Weather Conditions:

Birds Spotted / Quantity:

Birds Seen but Not Identified:
(Description)

Interesting Events:

Video Images Taken:
(File Name)

Notes / Bird Photo:

Bird Photo / Sketch:

Date:

Location: _____

Habitat: _____

GPS Co-ordinates: _____

Weather Conditions: _____

_____

Birds Spotted / Quantity: _____

_____

_____

_____

_____

Birds Seen but Not Identified: _____
(Description)

_____

_____

_____

_____

Interesting Events: _____

_____

_____

_____

Video Images Taken: _____
(File Name)

Notes / Bird Photo:

Bird Photo / Sketch:

Date:

Location:

Habitat:

GPS Co-ordinates:

Weather Conditions:

Birds Spotted / Quantity:

Birds Seen but Not Identified:
(Description)

Interesting Events:

Video Images Taken:
(File Name)

Notes / Bird Photo:

Bird Photo / Sketch:

Date:

Location:

Habitat:

GPS Co-ordinates:

Weather Conditions:

Birds Spotted / Quantity:

Birds Seen but Not Identified:
(Description)

Interesting Events:

Video Images Taken:
(File Name)

Notes / Bird Photo:

Bird Photo / Sketch:

Date:

Location:

Habitat:

GPS Co-ordinates:

Weather Conditions:

Birds Spotted / Quantity:

Birds Seen but Not Identified:
(Description)

Interesting Events:

Video Images Taken:
(File Name)

Notes / Bird Photo:

Bird Photo / Sketch:

Date:

Location:

Habitat:

GPS Co-ordinates:

Weather Conditions:

Birds Spotted / Quantity:

Birds Seen but Not Identified:
(Description)

Interesting Events:

Video Images Taken:
(File Name)

Notes / Bird Photo:

Bird Photo / Sketch:

Date:

Location:

Habitat:

GPS Co-ordinates:

Weather Conditions:

Birds Spotted / Quantity:

Birds Seen but Not Identified:
(Description)

Interesting Events:

Video Images Taken:
(File Name)

Notes / Bird Photo:

Bird Photo / Sketch:

Date:

Location:

Habitat:

GPS Co-ordinates:

Weather Conditions:

Birds Spotted / Quantity:

Birds Seen but Not Identified:
(Description)

Interesting Events:

Video Images Taken:
(File Name)

Notes / Bird Photo:

Bird Photo / Sketch:

Date:

Location: _____

Habitat: _____

GPS Co-ordinates: _____

Weather Conditions: _____

Birds Spotted / Quantity: _____

_____

_____

_____

_____

Birds Seen but Not Identified: _____
(Description)

_____

_____

_____

_____

Interesting Events: _____

_____

_____

_____

Video Images Taken: _____
(File Name)

Notes / Bird Photo:

Bird Photo / Sketch:

Date:

Location:

Habitat:

GPS Co-ordinates:

Weather Conditions:

Birds Spotted / Quantity:

Birds Seen but Not Identified:
(Description)

Interesting Events:

Video Images Taken:
(File Name)

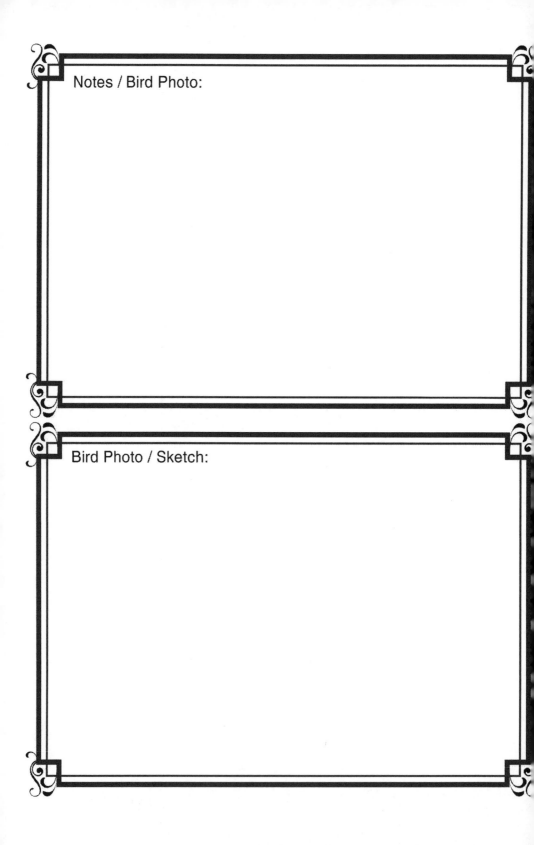

Notes / Bird Photo:

Bird Photo / Sketch:

Date:

Location: _____

Habitat: _____

GPS Co-ordinates: _____

Weather Conditions: _____

Birds Spotted / Quantity: _____

_____

_____

_____

_____

Birds Seen but Not Identified: _____
(Description)

_____

_____

_____

_____

Interesting Events: _____

_____

_____

_____

Video Images Taken: _____
(File Name)

Notes / Bird Photo:

Bird Photo / Sketch:

Date:

Location:

Habitat:

GPS Co-ordinates:

Weather Conditions:

Birds Spotted / Quantity:

Birds Seen but Not Identified:
(Description)

Interesting Events:

Video Images Taken:
(File Name)

Notes / Bird Photo:

Bird Photo / Sketch:

Date:

Location: _____

Habitat: _____

GPS Co-ordinates: _____

Weather Conditions: _____

Birds Spotted / Quantity: _____

_____

_____

_____

_____

Birds Seen but Not Identified: _____
(Description)

_____

_____

_____

_____

Interesting Events: _____

_____

_____

_____

Video Images Taken: _____
(File Name)

Notes / Bird Photo:

Bird Photo / Sketch:

Date:

Location:

Habitat:

GPS Co-ordinates:

Weather Conditions:

Birds Spotted / Quantity:

Birds Seen but Not Identified:
(Description)

Interesting Events:

Video Images Taken:
(File Name)

Notes / Bird Photo:

Bird Photo / Sketch:

Date:

Location:

Habitat:

GPS Co-ordinates:

Weather Conditions:

Birds Spotted / Quantity:

Birds Seen but Not Identified:
(Description)

Interesting Events:

Video Images Taken:
(File Name)

Notes / Bird Photo:

Bird Photo / Sketch:

Date:

Location:

Habitat:

GPS Co-ordinates:

Weather Conditions:

Birds Spotted / Quantity:

Birds Seen but Not Identified:
(Description)

Interesting Events:

Video Images Taken:
(File Name)

Notes / Bird Photo:

Bird Photo / Sketch:

Date:

Location:

Habitat:

GPS Co-ordinates:

Weather Conditions:

Birds Spotted / Quantity:

Birds Seen but Not Identified:
(Description)

Interesting Events:

Video Images Taken:
(File Name)

Notes / Bird Photo:

Bird Photo / Sketch:

Date:

Location: _____

Habitat: _____

GPS Co-ordinates: _____

Weather Conditions: _____

Birds Spotted / Quantity: _____

_____

_____

_____

_____

Birds Seen but Not Identified: _____
(Description)

_____

_____

_____

_____

Interesting Events: _____

_____

_____

_____

Video Images Taken: _____
(File Name)

Notes / Bird Photo:

Bird Photo / Sketch:

Date:

Location:

Habitat:

GPS Co-ordinates:

Weather Conditions:

Birds Spotted / Quantity:

Birds Seen but Not Identified:
(Description)

Interesting Events:

Video Images Taken:
(File Name)

Notes / Bird Photo:

Bird Photo / Sketch:

Date:

Location:

Habitat:

GPS Co-ordinates:

Weather Conditions:

Birds Spotted / Quantity:

Birds Seen but Not Identified:
(Description)

Interesting Events:

Video Images Taken:
(File Name)

Notes / Bird Photo:

Bird Photo / Sketch:

Date:

Location:

Habitat:

GPS Co-ordinates:

Weather Conditions:

Birds Spotted / Quantity:

Birds Seen but Not Identified:
(Description)

Interesting Events:

Video Images Taken:
(File Name)

Notes / Bird Photo:

Bird Photo / Sketch:

Date:

Location:

Habitat:

GPS Co-ordinates:

Weather Conditions:

Birds Spotted / Quantity:

Birds Seen but Not Identified:
(Description)

Interesting Events:

Video Images Taken:
(File Name)

Notes / Bird Photo:

Bird Photo / Sketch:

Date:

Location:

Habitat:

GPS Co-ordinates:

Weather Conditions:

Birds Spotted / Quantity:

Birds Seen but Not Identified:
(Description)

Interesting Events:

Video Images Taken:
(File Name)

Notes / Bird Photo:

Bird Photo / Sketch:

Date:

Location:

Habitat:

GPS Co-ordinates:

Weather Conditions:

Birds Spotted / Quantity:

Birds Seen but Not Identified:
(Description)

Interesting Events:

Video Images Taken:
(File Name)

Notes / Bird Photo:

Bird Photo / Sketch:

Date:

Location:

Habitat:

GPS Co-ordinates:

Weather Conditions:

Birds Spotted / Quantity:

Birds Seen but Not Identified:
(Description)

Interesting Events:

Video Images Taken:
(File Name)

Notes / Bird Photo:

Bird Photo / Sketch:

Date:

Location:

Habitat:

GPS Co-ordinates:

Weather Conditions:

Birds Spotted / Quantity:

Birds Seen but Not Identified:
(Description)

Interesting Events:

Video Images Taken:
(File Name)

Notes / Bird Photo:

Bird Photo / Sketch:

Date:

Location:

Habitat:

GPS Co-ordinates:

Weather Conditions:

Birds Spotted / Quantity:

Birds Seen but Not Identified:
(Description)

Interesting Events:

Video Images Taken:
(File Name)

Notes / Bird Photo:

Bird Photo / Sketch:

Date:

Location: _____

Habitat: _____

GPS Co-ordinates: _____

Weather Conditions: _____

_____

Birds Spotted / Quantity: _____

_____

_____

_____

_____

_____

Birds Seen but Not Identified: _____
(Description)

_____

_____

_____

_____

_____

Interesting Events: _____

_____

_____

_____

Video Images Taken: _____
(File Name)

Notes / Bird Photo:

Bird Photo / Sketch:

Date:

Location:

Habitat:

GPS Co-ordinates:

Weather Conditions:

Birds Spotted / Quantity:

Birds Seen but Not Identified:
(Description)

Interesting Events:

Video Images Taken:
(File Name)

Notes / Bird Photo:

Bird Photo / Sketch:

Date:

Location:

Habitat:

GPS Co-ordinates:

Weather Conditions:

Birds Spotted / Quantity:

Birds Seen but Not Identified:
(Description)

Interesting Events:

Video Images Taken:
(File Name)

Notes / Bird Photo:

Bird Photo / Sketch:

Date:

Location: _____

Habitat: _____

GPS Co-ordinates: _____

Weather Conditions: _____

_____

Birds Spotted / Quantity: _____

_____

_____

_____

_____

_____

Birds Seen but Not Identified: _____
(Description)

_____

_____

_____

_____

_____

Interesting Events: _____

_____

_____

_____

Video Images Taken: _____
(File Name)

Notes / Bird Photo:

Bird Photo / Sketch:

Date:

Location: _____

Habitat: _____

GPS Co-ordinates: _____

Weather Conditions: _____

_____

Birds Spotted / Quantity: _____

_____

_____

_____

_____

_____

Birds Seen but Not Identified: _____
(Description)

_____

_____

_____

_____

Interesting Events: _____

_____

_____

_____

Video Images Taken: _____
(File Name)

Notes / Bird Photo:

Bird Photo / Sketch:

Date:

Location: _____

Habitat: _____

GPS Co-ordinates: _____

Weather Conditions: _____

Birds Spotted / Quantity: _____

_____

_____

_____

_____

_____

Birds Seen but Not Identified: _____
(Description)

_____

_____

_____

_____

_____

Interesting Events: _____

_____

_____

_____

Video Images Taken: _____
(File Name)

Notes / Bird Photo:

Bird Photo / Sketch:

Date:

Location:

Habitat:

GPS Co-ordinates:

Weather Conditions:

Birds Spotted / Quantity:

Birds Seen but Not Identified:
(Description)

Interesting Events:

Video Images Taken:
(File Name)

Notes / Bird Photo:

Bird Photo / Sketch:

Date:

Location:

Habitat:

GPS Co-ordinates:

Weather Conditions:

Birds Spotted / Quantity:

Birds Seen but Not Identified:
(Description)

Interesting Events:

Video Images Taken:
(File Name)

Notes / Bird Photo:

Bird Photo / Sketch:

Date:

Location:

Habitat:

GPS Co-ordinates:

Weather Conditions:

Birds Spotted / Quantity:

Birds Seen but Not Identified:
(Description)

Interesting Events:

Video Images Taken:
(File Name)

Notes / Bird Photo:

Bird Photo / Sketch:

Date:

Location: _____

Habitat: _____

GPS Co-ordinates: _____

Weather Conditions: _____

Birds Spotted / Quantity: _____

_____

_____

_____

_____

_____

Birds Seen but Not Identified: _____
(Description)

_____

_____

_____

_____

_____

Interesting Events: _____

_____

_____

_____

Video Images Taken: _____
(File Name)

Notes / Bird Photo:

Bird Photo / Sketch:

Date:

Location: _____

Habitat: _____

GPS Co-ordinates: _____

Weather Conditions: _____

_____

Birds Spotted / Quantity: _____

_____

_____

_____

_____

_____

Birds Seen but Not Identified: _____
(Description)

_____

_____

_____

_____

_____

Interesting Events: _____

_____

_____

_____

Video Images Taken: _____
(File Name)

Notes / Bird Photo:

Bird Photo / Sketch:

Date:

Location:

Habitat:

GPS Co-ordinates:

Weather Conditions:

Birds Spotted / Quantity:

Birds Seen but Not Identified:
(Description)

Interesting Events:

Video Images Taken:
(File Name)

Notes / Bird Photo:

Bird Photo / Sketch:

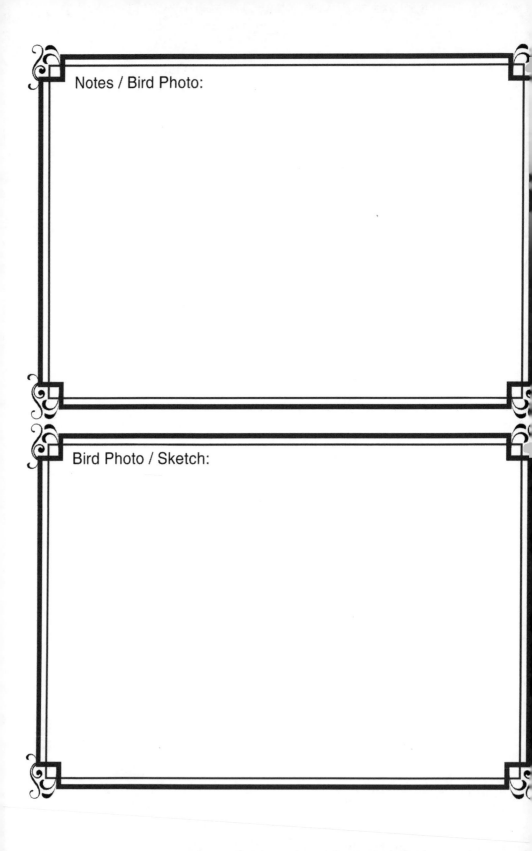

Date:

Location:

Habitat:

GPS Co-ordinates:

Weather Conditions:

Birds Spotted / Quantity:

Birds Seen but Not Identified:
(Description)

Interesting Events:

Video Images Taken:
(File Name)

Notes / Bird Photo:

Bird Photo / Sketch:

Date:

Location:

Habitat:

GPS Co-ordinates:

Weather Conditions:

Birds Spotted / Quantity:

Birds Seen but Not Identified:
(Description)

Interesting Events:

Video Images Taken:
(File Name)

Notes / Bird Photo:

Bird Photo / Sketch:

Date:

Location: _____

Habitat: _____

GPS Co-ordinates: _____

Weather Conditions: _____

_____

Birds Spotted / Quantity: _____

_____

_____

_____

_____

_____

Birds Seen but Not Identified: _____
(Description)

_____

_____

_____

_____

_____

Interesting Events: _____

_____

_____

_____

Video Images Taken: _____
(File Name)

Notes / Bird Photo:

Bird Photo / Sketch:

Date:

Location: _____

Habitat: _____

GPS Co-ordinates: _____

Weather Conditions: _____

Birds Spotted / Quantity: _____

Birds Seen but Not Identified: _____
(Description)

Interesting Events: _____

Video Images Taken: _____
(File Name)

Notes / Bird Photo:

Bird Photo / Sketch:

Date:

Location:

Habitat:

GPS Co-ordinates:

Weather Conditions:

Birds Spotted / Quantity:

Birds Seen but Not Identified:
(Description)

Interesting Events:

Video Images Taken:
(File Name)

Notes / Bird Photo:

Bird Photo / Sketch:

Date:

Location: _____

Habitat: _____

GPS Co-ordinates: _____

Weather Conditions: _____

Birds Spotted / Quantity: _____

_____

_____

_____

_____

Birds Seen but Not Identified: _____
(Description)

_____

_____

_____

_____

Interesting Events: _____

_____

_____

_____

Video Images Taken: _____
(File Name)

Notes / Bird Photo:

Bird Photo / Sketch:

Date:

Location: _____

Habitat: _____

GPS Co-ordinates: _____

Weather Conditions: _____

Birds Spotted / Quantity: _____

_____

_____

_____

_____

_____

Birds Seen but Not Identified: _____
(Description)

_____

_____

_____

_____

_____

Interesting Events: _____

_____

_____

_____

Video Images Taken: _____
(File Name)

Notes / Bird Photo:

Bird Photo / Sketch:

Date:

Location:

Habitat:

GPS Co-ordinates:

Weather Conditions:

Birds Spotted / Quantity:

Birds Seen but Not Identified:
(Description)

Interesting Events:

Video Images Taken:
(File Name)

Notes / Bird Photo:

Bird Photo / Sketch:

Date:

Location:

Habitat:

GPS Co-ordinates:

Weather Conditions:

Birds Spotted / Quantity:

Birds Seen but Not Identified:
(Description)

Interesting Events:

Video Images Taken:
(File Name)

Notes / Bird Photo:

Bird Photo / Sketch:

Date:

Location:

Habitat:

GPS Co-ordinates:

Weather Conditions:

Birds Spotted / Quantity:

Birds Seen but Not Identified:
(Description)

Interesting Events:

Video Images Taken:
(File Name)

Notes / Bird Photo:

Bird Photo / Sketch:

Date:

Location:

Habitat:

GPS Co-ordinates:

Weather Conditions:

Birds Spotted / Quantity:

Birds Seen but Not Identified:
(Description)

Interesting Events:

Video Images Taken:
(File Name)

Notes / Bird Photo:

Bird Photo / Sketch:

Date:

Location: _____

Habitat: _____

GPS Co-ordinates: _____

Weather Conditions: _____

Birds Spotted / Quantity: _____

_____

_____

_____

_____

_____

Birds Seen but Not Identified: _____
(Description)

_____

_____

_____

_____

_____

Interesting Events: _____

_____

_____

_____

Video Images Taken: _____
(File Name)

Notes / Bird Photo:

Bird Photo / Sketch:

Date:

Location: _____

Habitat: _____

GPS Co-ordinates: _____

Weather Conditions: _____

_____

Birds Spotted / Quantity: _____

_____

_____

_____

_____

Birds Seen but Not Identified: _____
(Description)

_____

_____

_____

_____

Interesting Events: _____

_____

_____

_____

Video Images Taken: _____
(File Name)

Notes / Bird Photo:

Bird Photo / Sketch:

Date:

Location: _____

Habitat: _____

GPS Co-ordinates: _____

Weather Conditions: _____

_____

Birds Spotted / Quantity: _____

_____

_____

_____

_____

Birds Seen but Not Identified: _____
(Description)

_____

_____

_____

_____

Interesting Events: _____

_____

_____

_____

Video Images Taken: _____
(File Name)

Notes / Bird Photo:

Bird Photo / Sketch:

Date:

Location:

Habitat:

GPS Co-ordinates:

Weather Conditions:

Birds Spotted / Quantity:

Birds Seen but Not Identified:
(Description)

Interesting Events:

Video Images Taken:
(File Name)

Manufactured by Amazon.ca
Bolton, ON